THEODORE ROOSEVELT

PRESIDENTIAL ✦ LEADERS

THEODORE ROOSEVELT

STEPHANIE SAMMARTINO MCPHERSON

LERNER PUBLICATIONS COMPANY/MINNEAPOLIS

For my parents, Angelo and Marion Sammartino

Special thanks to my editor Mary Winget for her help and
suggestions, to Angelo Sammartino and Richard McPherson
for sharing their ideas, and to Becky Raymond for sharing her
expertise on the Panama Canal.

Lerner Publications Company
A division of Lerner Publishing Group
241 First Avenue North
Minneapolis, MN 55401 U.S.A.

Website address: www.lernerbooks.com

Library of Congress Cataloging-in-Publication Data

McPherson, Stephanie Sammartino.
    Theodore Roosevelt / by Stephanie Sammartino McPherson.
      p.   cm. — (Presidential leaders)
    Includes bibliographical references and index.
    ISBN: 0–8225–0999–7 (lib. bdg. : alk. paper)
      1. Roosevelt, Theodore, 1858–1919—Juvenile literature. 2. Presidents—United States—
  Biography—Juvenile literature. I. Title. II. Series.
    E757.M46 2005
    973.91'1'092—dc22   2004002596

Manufactured in the United States of America
1 2 3 4 5 6 – JR – 10 09 08 07 06 05

CONTENTS

Roosevelt (left) was a great lover of nature and adventure.
He stands with naturalist John Muir (right) atop a mountain in 1903.

INTRODUCTION

URGENT SUMMONS

It's a dreadful thing to come into the presidency this way, but it would be a far worse thing to be morbid about it.

—Theodore Roosevelt, to his friend
Henry Cabot Lodge

There was never a question of turning back. Vice President Theodore Roosevelt and his companions had spent hours climbing through heavy rain. Their feet slipped on the wet rocks. They could barely see through the fog. But Roosevelt had always welcomed physical challenges—whether it was boxing, swimming, or buffalo hunting in the Badlands of the Dakota Territory. To him, such adventures were "bully"—his favorite word to describe something that excited him. No amount of bad weather was going to keep the vice president of the United States from reaching the top of Mount Marcy, the highest peak in New York's Adirondack Mountains.

With a final spurt of energy, the drenched men scrambled onto the summit. Suddenly, the sun broke through the clouds, and the climbers could see for miles. "Beautiful country!" Roosevelt exclaimed as his eyes swept the wooded slopes.

The view didn't last long. Thick clouds blotted the sun again as the small party descended to a shelf of rock. Roosevelt was delighted with his outing and hungry for lunch.

Then he saw a guide hiking up the mountain. When the messenger reached the ledge, he handed the vice president a telegram. A quick scan of its contents confirmed Roosevelt's worst fears. President William McKinley's condition was declining rapidly. One week earlier, on September 6, 1901, an assassin had shot the president while he was visiting Buffalo, New York. Steeling himself to remain calm, Roosevelt struggled down the mountain.

By six o'clock that evening, he had reached the lodge where his family was staying. No further word had come, and he began to think McKinley might not be in as much danger as he had suspected. Somewhat uncertainly, Roosevelt prepared to go to bed.

Several hours later, the unwelcome news arrived. President McKinley's condition was desperate. Roosevelt would have to leave for Buffalo at once. Vigorously, Roosevelt heaved himself onto the wagon that would take him to the nearest railroad station, which was about forty miles away.

Steep drops bordered sharp curves in the road. "Hurry up! Go faster!" Roosevelt shouted. Even when the driver urged caution, Roosevelt cried, "Push ahead! If you're not afraid, I am not!"

A small gathering of people waited at the station as the wagon clattered up to the train depot. Roosevelt's secretary, William Loeb, stepped forward to hand him a telegram. The news was no surprise, but seeing it in black and white made it official. McKinley had died at 2:15 that morning. Theodore Roosevelt—writer, war hero, and former governor of New York—was the new president of the United States. At forty-two, he was the youngest man ever to assume such responsibility.

CHAPTER ONE

YOUNG ADVENTURER

It is hard drudgery to make one's body,
but I know you will do it.
—Theodore Roosevelt Sr. to his son

Theodore Roosevelt hadn't always been strong and brave. Long before he climbed mountains, he was simply Teedie, a pale, sickly boy who lived with his family in a brownstone mansion in New York City. Teedie had every comfort and advantage that wealth could buy. But he was so prone to asthma that he often needed help to breathe. He never forgot the nights his father wrapped him in blankets, hoisted him into the carriage, and raced through the streets. The air rushing noisily past forced itself into Teedie's lungs.

A FAMILY DIVIDED

Despite his health problems, Teedie was bright, alert, and full of imagination. Born October 27, 1858, he wasn't even three years old when the Civil War (1861–1865) broke out in April

Roosevelt in 1862, one year after the start of the Civil War, at the age of 4

✧ ─────────────

1861. Although Teedie was too young to understand what the war was about, he soon realized that his family was split down the middle. Father, who came from an important and well-respected Dutch family, wanted the North to win the war. Teedie's mother, Mittie, who grew up on a plantation in Georgia, supported the South.

Two of Mittie's brothers were fighting in the Confederate (Southern) navy. She couldn't bear for her husband to take up arms against her relatives. Respecting her wishes, Theodore Roosevelt Sr. did not join the army. Instead, he paid a substitute to take his place. Theodore went to Washington, D.C., to work for laws that would help the soldiers' families.

After Theodore left, Teedie's health worsened. He had always counted on his father to make things all right, and he missed him greatly. But even without his father, Teedie's house was full of people. He had an older sister Anna (nicknamed Bamie), a younger brother Elliott, and a baby sister named Corinne. In addition, Grandmother Bulloch lived with the family. So did Aunt Anna, his mother's sister, who told wonderful stories about life in the South. One by one, Aunt Anna also taught the children to read and do arithmetic.

During the war, Teedie's mother, grandmother, and aunt made packages with clothes, medicine, and other supplies to send to friends and relatives in the South. Sometimes Bamie and Teedie helped to stuff the bundles. The children only knew that the parcels would be secretly slipped to strangers who would somehow get them past the blockades the Union navy maintained around Southern ports.

Teedie thought it sounded exciting and mysterious. He made up a game called "running the blockade" that he played with Bamie in Central Park. Bamie pretended to be the blockade runner, slipping through the Union ships surrounding Southern ports, and Teedie was one of the Union ships. Over and over again, Teedie's Union "boat" captured Bamie.

On April 3, 1865, General Robert E. Lee, commander of the Southern troops, surrendered to General Ulysses S. Grant, commander of the Northern troops, at Appomatox Court House in Virginia.

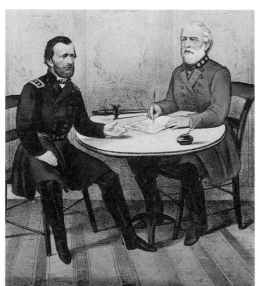

✧ ——————————

The Civil War ended in 1865 when General Robert E. Lee (right) surrendered to General Ulysses S. Grant (left).

Union soldiers advance from the right while Confederate soldiers hold their positions on the left during the Battle of Lookout Mountain in Tennessee in 1863.

THE CIVIL WAR

The Civil War divided the United States on the issue of slavery. The South believed that the states had the right to allow or to outlaw slavery. Many people in the North felt there should be no slavery anywhere in the United States. Eventually, the Southern states decided to break away from the Union and form their own government—the Confederate States of America. Northern, or Union, soldiers fought to keep the nation together and to end slavery. The North won the war, and slavery was outlawed throughout the nation.

Less than one week later, the nation was plunged into mourning when President Abraham Lincoln was assassinated. Lincoln's funeral procession passed right through New York City. Teedie and his brother watched the sorrowful scene from the second floor of their grandfather's house just blocks away from their own.

With the war over, Teedie's father came home for good. Teedie later said that his father was "the best man I ever knew." All over the city, children depended on Theodore's kindness and generosity. He started several badly needed charitable organizations, such as the Children's Aid Society, located foster homes for street children whenever possible, and took time to befriend the youngsters and offer advice. On holidays, Theodore often took his children to help with dinner at the Newsboys' Lodging House, which he had also helped establish.

IN SEARCH OF ADVENTURE

Although he was still frail, Teedie wanted to be brave. Like Aunt Anna, Teedie was a wonderful teller of tales. He liked to describe jungles and fierce battles between small boys and wild, mysterious animals. Unlike the heroes in his stories, Teedie wasn't bold. "I was nervous and timid," he later admitted of his boyhood. But he longed for adventure.

One day as he walked up Broadway past the outdoor market, he spied a dead seal stretched on a plank of wood. The sleek, shiny animal reminded him of the great, wide world waiting to be explored. Every day Teedie hurried to see if the seal was still there. He measured it and studied it from every angle. Eventually, he got the owner to give him the seal's skull. With this great prize, Teedie and two cousins started the Roosevelt Museum of Natural History.

Teedie always loved to explore nature. Summers in rural New Jersey gave him plenty of chances for great outdoor fun. Birds and other wildlife fascinated Teedie as he shuffled through the woods. He loved to collect nuts and apples. Soon Teedie was collecting all sorts of specimens from bugs to reptiles. Visitors took to checking the water pitchers for snakes, and a maid complained about the snapping turtle tied to the kitchen sink. Although she supported his new passion, Teedie's mother was not amused when she found dead field mice stored in the icebox (a chest with blocks of ice to keep food cold). And one day when Teedie tipped his hat to a family friend on a streetcar, frogs jumped out.

Teedie was extremely happy with his museum and his books and his wonderful summers in the country. Then his parents made other plans. They announced that the family would spend a year traveling in Europe. Ten-year-old Teedie would have preferred to stay at home. But he enjoyed meeting his Confederate uncles who had moved to England after the war. Fascinated, Teedie listened to their talk of sea battles.

The Roosevelts kept a fast-paced schedule in Europe. Sometimes they visited dozens of tourist sites in a single day. What Teedie recalled most in later years, however, was escaping from the watchful eyes of his parents, running down hotel hallways, and throwing paper balls at the maids. Tired of sightseeing, he was thrilled when the family returned to New York.

Teedie was growing into a spirited, determined young man, interested in almost everything. But his asthma still left him coughing, wheezing, and gasping for breath. His father considered the situation and decided it was time for Teedie to take charge of his own health.

"Theodore," said his father, using his son's grown-up name, "you have the mind but not the body, and without the help of the body the mind cannot go as far as it should. You *must* make your body," he urged.

Teedie didn't hesitate even for a minute. "I will make my body," he promised.

CHAPTER TWO

FORGING A FUTURE

My life has such absurd contrasts. I live in the height of luxury; and then for a month will undergo really severe toil [work] and hardship— and enjoy both extremes almost equally.
—Theodore Roosevelt in his college diary

Teedie spent hours working out each day. His chest expanded, his muscles grew strong, and he suffered fewer bouts of asthma. Soon he felt healthy enough to add taxidermy lessons to his demanding schedule. Taxidermy is the science of stuffing and preserving dead animals for display. Some members of the family found it hard to share Teedie's newest interest. A smell of chemicals and dead birds surrounded Teedie like a cloud. Splotches of arsenic, a poisonous acid used in taxidermy, colored his hands.

Despite Teedie's untidy looks and unmistakable odor, his father gave him a shotgun so he could get more specimens for his collection. Teedie loved animals. Like many

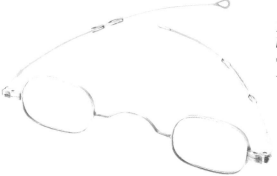

Roosevelt's first glasses may have looked like these, which were made in the late 1800s.

✧ ———————

scientists of the time, however, he believed it was all right—and even necessary—to kill animals in order to study them more closely. But no matter how carefully he aimed, all Teedie's shots missed their mark.

Then one day, Teedie was surprised to hear his friends read a message on a distant billboard. Was that blur he saw in the distance really a billboard? After that, his father took him to the eye doctor, and Teedie got his first pair of glasses. Suddenly, all sorts of fascinating details came into focus. "I had no idea how beautiful the world was until I got those spectacles," he recalled.

ADVENTURES AT HOME AND ABROAD

Teedie's glasses allowed him to appreciate the sights on the Roosevelts' second trip abroad. The family arrived in Liverpool, England, late in 1872 to visit the Confederate uncles again, then traveled through Europe. As far as Teedie was concerned, the best part of the trip came after crossing the Mediterranean Sea to Egypt. From there, the family cruised down the Nile River on a special boat called a dahabeah. The comfortable craft, with its awning-covered decks, was similar in design to vessels that had sailed the

Nile for four thousand years. Teedie loved it! He spent two hours each morning doing lessons. Then the boat stopped for some adventure onshore. Teedie spent hours bagging strange and exotic birds for his collection. Nothing seemed to faze Teedie—not the hot sun, the long distances, or the dangerous bogs that sucked at his ankles. When he returned to the dahabeah, he sat happily on deck and stuffed his birds.

Teedie grew so fast on the Nile voyage that his ankles and wrists soon stuck out of his clothes. Not once did he suffer from asthma. "I think I have enjoyed myself more this winter than ever before," he wrote to Edith Carow, one of his best friends.

———————————— ✧ ————————————

In Egypt Teedie climbed the outside of a pyramid and crawled through the narrow tunnels inside. In the photograph below, the Egyptian pyramids are seen behind the winding Nile River.

From Egypt the family went to the Holy Land (Palestine at that time) and then to Greece. Finally, they wound up at Dresden, Germany, where arrangements were made for Teedie and his younger brother to live with a family. Their parents hoped the boys would speak fluent German by the end of five months.

At first, the Minkowitz family found Teedie a little strange. They took away his arsenic and threw his mice out the window. But Fraulein (Miss) Anna, the oldest daughter, who tutored Teedie in German and arithmetic, soon discovered how smart and hardworking he was. "You need not be anxious about him," she told Teedie's mother as the family prepared to return to America. "He will surely one day be a great professor, or who knows, he may even become president of the United States."

The Roosevelts had a new, much larger house waiting for them when they arrived back in New York. Teedie had the whole attic for his museum and his gym. For the summers, the Roosevelts rented a big white house at Oyster Bay, by the ocean on Long Island. Surrounded by cousins and friends, Teedie went hunting, riding, swimming, and sailing. But his special companion was Edith Carow. As Teedie continued his outdoor adventures and studied for his college entrance tests, their friendship deepened. Like Teedie, Edith loved to read. The last summer before Teedie left for college, the two spent many hours talking and sharing their interests.

COLLEGE MAN

Teedie wasn't quite eighteen when his father took him to the railroad station to set off for Harvard University in

Harvard Hall at Harvard University in 1870,
just a few years before Roosevelt started college there

Massachusetts in 1876. "Take care of your morals first," his father had advised. "Your health next and finally your studies."

Roosevelt (who no longer considered himself Teedie) paid careful attention to all three. From boxing to poetry readings, he enjoyed almost everything about college. His classmates didn't quite know what to make of the wiry young man with the clipped, high-pitched voice and boundless energy. At times, neither did his teachers. Theodore asked so many questions in class that one professor exclaimed, "Now look here, Roosevelt, let me talk! I'm running this course!"

Roosevelt had an excellent memory and learned quickly. He got good grades and enjoyed reading books on many subjects. While he was reading, he often forgot everything around him. One day while he was comfortably reading by the fire, Roosevelt was roused by a strange smell. The soles of his shoes had caught fire!

Roosevelt's life was just about perfect until February 1878, when he received a telegram telling him to come home at once. Although Roosevelt knew his father was ill, he had thought he was improving. By the time Roosevelt reached New York, his father had died. "He was everything to me," the grief-stricken young man wrote. Roosevelt put on a brave face when he returned to Harvard. He tried to forget his sadness in hard work and exercise, but at night he filled pages of his diary with his sorrow.

Still in mourning, Roosevelt continued his whirlwind pace that long summer—riding, hunting, and rowing. When Edith Carow came to visit

✧ ————————

Roosevelt poses in his deerskin hunting suit. He spent part of the summer of 1878 exploring the Maine wilderness.

at Oyster Bay, Roosevelt took her sailing and picking water lilies. He valued Edith's goodness, intelligent conversation, and quiet dignity. Then they quarreled. Although neither one ever explained the disagreement, both were strong willed, even stubborn.

LOVE AT FIRST SIGHT

Roosevelt felt as much at home in fashionable parlors as he did in the wilderness. When school started again, he visited the home of a wealthy classmate, where he met a beautiful seventeen-year-old girl named Alice Lee. By Thanksgiving he knew that he wanted to marry her. But Alice was not nearly so sure of her feelings for Roosevelt. With

Alice Lee Roosevelt

the same determination he summoned for all his goals, Roosevelt set out to win Alice's love. The first time he proposed, she turned him down. But he continued to visit and to take her on outings.

Finally, Roosevelt's efforts paid off. Alice agreed to marry him. "I am so happy that I dare not trust my own happiness," Roosevelt wrote in his diary. He was bursting with all sorts of plans. In the midst of excited preparations for his graduation and wedding, he was also writing a book, *The Naval War of 1812*. Perhaps, his Confederate uncles had inspired his fascination with the sea. The exciting literary project tugged at his sense of adventure, courage, and patriotism.

Nothing was going to stand in the way of Roosevelt's happiness and success—certainly not any health problems. But during a routine exam, his doctor detected an irregular heartbeat. The doctor advised Roosevelt to give up the hiking, swimming, and rowing that he loved. He even suggested Roosevelt be careful climbing stairs if he wished to live a long life.

"Doctor," Roosevelt replied, "I am going to do all the things you tell me not to do. If I've got to live the sort of life you have described, I don't care how short it is." He promised himself he would work as hard as he could until he was sixty.

Instead of taking it easy, Roosevelt went on a hunting trip through the Midwest with his brother. He was drenched by sudden downpours, bitten by a snake, and troubled again by asthma. Both his guns broke, and he fell from a wagon onto his head. But it took more than snake venom or a sore head to get Roosevelt down. He pronounced the trip "very good fun."

Back in civilization again, Roosevelt could hardly wait to see Alice—and to shower her with gifts. The wedding took place on October 27, 1880, Roosevelt's twenty-second birthday. After a two-week honeymoon at Oyster Bay, the young couple returned to New York, where they frequently dined out and attended fashionable balls and the theater.

THE NAVAL WAR OF 1812

Long hours of research and writing paid off for Roosevelt. In 1882 his book *The Naval War of 1812* received rave reviews. Although it was difficult reading, it was thorough and brilliant. Soon it became a naval textbook. In fact, the Navy Department ordered a copy for every ship in the U.S. fleet.

Roosevelt's first book was about the War of 1812 (1812-1815), which was fought between the United States and Great Britain.

A NEW INTEREST

No matter what late event he'd enjoyed the previous night, Roosevelt was up early to go to Columbia Law School. As a first-year student, he brought his usual enthusiasm to class. But the more he learned, the more he felt that certain aspects of the law were not fair. Roosevelt was always jumping up to protest something or to make a point. He felt strongly that laws should provide justice for everyone—not just wealthy businesses or large companies.

Although his studies, his social life, and the new book he was writing kept him busy, Roosevelt longed for more activity. Slowly, another interest took shape in his mind. He knew it was something wealthy and fashionable men usually avoided. But Roosevelt was curious, and he was not going to let custom tell him what he could or could not do. He was determined to explore the world of politics.

CHAPTER THREE

WHO'S THE DUDE?

I have never believed it did any good to flinch
or yield for any blow, nor does it lighten the
pain to cease from working.

—Theodore Roosevelt to
Anna "Bamie" Roosevelt

In his formal black coat and top hat, Theodore Roosevelt stood in sharp contrast to his surroundings. Morton Hall, a large, shabby room over a saloon, was filled with cigar smoke and stained with tobacco juice. Everything about Roosevelt, from his upper-class accent to his fancy eyeglass, plainly declared that he did not belong in such grimy surroundings. The regulars who assembled at the Twenty-first District Republican Association eyed Roosevelt suspiciously. Politics was a rough-and-tumble business. They didn't think Roosevelt belonged in politics any more than his society friends did.

Ignoring their doubts, Roosevelt kept coming to the meetings. If he had a formal social engagement for the evening, he would arrive in his fancy clothes. The other men got used to it. Despite his appearance, Roosevelt was not soft or snobbish. He was tough, smart, and ambitious. Soon a politician named Joe Murray decided that Roosevelt might prove a useful ally. The election for a representative to the state assembly (lawmaking body) was coming up. Was Roosevelt interested in seeking the nomination? Murray asked. After a brief hesitation, Roosevelt decided he was.

Thanks to Murray's careful strategy, the members of the Twenty-first District Republican Association selected Roosevelt as their candidate. Nine days later, Roosevelt cast his vote early in the morning and hurried to the library to work on his naval history. Later, a caller arrived at his home "wishing to meet the rising star." Roosevelt realized that he had won the election. On January 2,

1882, he arrived in Albany, the state capital, to take up his new duties.

YOUNG ASSEMBLYMAN

All eyes focused on Roosevelt as he burst into the assembly chamber that first evening. In one hand, he held a gold-topped cane, in the other, a silk hat. The tails of his fancy coat reached almost to his shoes, and according to one observer, "His trousers were as tight as a tailor could make them."

"Who's the dude?" The question rippled through the room, while some members had to fight back laughter at Roosevelt's ridiculous appearance.

It didn't take long, however, for the other assemblymen to see that Roosevelt was no mere fashion plate. He wasn't afraid to call for an investigation of a well-known judge whom he believed guilty of fraud. He wanted honesty in government and business, and he was willing to fight for any cause he believed just. Sometimes he got carried away when he had something to say. "He was just like a Jack coming out of the box," a fellow assemblyman recalled. "He yelled and pounded his desk.... He was a perfect nuisance." But Roosevelt didn't mind as long as he made his point.

No one had ever seen an assemblyman like Roosevelt. Even the way Roosevelt talked was different. Fellow assemblymen never forgot the tireless determination with which Roosevelt demanded attention. "Mr. Spee-kar! Mr. Spee-kar!" he called repeatedly. When the chairman finally recognized Roosevelt, his high-pitched, clipped words echoed through the room.

Roosevelt never tired of investigating issues or debating bills. And he wasn't afraid to admit mistakes or change his mind. At first, he opposed a bill that would ban the making of cigars in slum apartments. Then he went on a tour to see the working conditions for himself. Roosevelt was horrified by the stuffy, dirty, overcrowded rooms where even children were busy rolling tobacco. Disease spread quickly in such unhealthy quarters. After his firsthand look, Roosevelt worked hard to get the bill passed.

When he had been in the assembly several months, Roosevelt bought a brownstone house in New York City, where he spent his weekends with Alice. By the next summer, the young couple had also decided to build a big house at Oyster Bay on Long Island Sound. Roosevelt knew exactly what he wanted—a large porch, his own library, big fireplaces for stout logs. He hoped to fill up the ten bedrooms with lots of children. Alice was expecting a baby in February 1884.

ON THE TRAIL OF BUFFALO

Roosevelt could never go long without craving outdoor adventure. Before running in his third election campaign, he decided to try buffalo hunting in the Dakota Badlands, in present-day South Dakota. The train left him at the tiny town of Little Missouri in the middle of the night. All he could see by the moonlight was sagebrush and some dark huts. In daylight, Roosevelt was impressed by the dramatic landscape with its vast empty spaces, branching creeks, and clumps of wildflowers. Wasting little time, he hired a guide and set off after buffalo.

*Plenty of buffalo roamed the territory that later became South Dakota,
but it took Roosevelt two weeks of hunting to get one.*

For almost two weeks, the men rode through the
wilds. Rain beat down. Their supplies ran low until all
they had were biscuits and rainwater. The guide was eager
to turn back, but not Roosevelt. "By Godfrey, but this is
fun!" he cried. When Roosevelt finally got his buffalo, he
whooped, broke into an excited war dance, and gave the
guide one hundred dollars. The entire Badlands experience
thrilled him so much that he decided to try his hand at
ranching. Before he went home, he invested fourteen
thousand dollars, an enormous amount of money, in a herd
of cattle.

A CURSE ON HIS HOUSE

Easily winning reelection that November, Roosevelt returned to the assembly in Albany while his wife awaited the birth of their child in New York City. For the sake of companionship, she moved in with Roosevelt's mother and older sister. Every weekend, Roosevelt took the five-hour train ride to see them. He had barely returned from one visit when he received a telegram in Albany. Alice had given birth to a baby girl on February 12, 1884. Joyfully, Roosevelt shared the news with colleagues and friends. He could scarcely wait to see his new daughter. Then a second telegram arrived. Alice had taken ill suddenly. Roosevelt was needed at home immediately.

Tired and frightened, Roosevelt arrived home late at night. His brother Elliott met him at the door. "There is a curse on this house," he said hopelessly. "Mother is dying, and Alice is dying too."

Numb with anxiety, Roosevelt raced upstairs where Alice lay semiconscious, suffering from a kidney disease that had gone undetected during her pregnancy. Roosevelt cradled his young wife tenderly until it was time to say a final good-bye to his mother. He was with Mittie when she died of a sudden, severe case of typhoid. Later that afternoon, Alice died in his arms.

Roosevelt's grief was boundless. He sat stunned through the double funeral. "He does not know what he does or says," remarked his old tutor. But Roosevelt despised weakness. Within three days, he had pulled himself together enough to return to Albany. He left his infant daughter with his sister, and he refused to talk about his loss. He threw himself into his work. "I think I should go mad if I were not employed," he wrote to a friend.

That summer Theodore Roosevelt attended the Republican presidential convention in Chicago, Illinois, where he worked tirelessly for the nomination of George Edmunds. When his candidate failed to be selected, he headed back to the Badlands. He would try to forget his sorrow in the Wild West.

CHAPTER FOUR

SECOND CHANCES

There were all kinds of things of which I was afraid at first, ranging from grizzly bears to 'mean' horses and gunfighters; but by acting as if I was not afraid I gradually ceased to be afraid.

—Theodore Roosevelt, reflecting on his life as a rancher

The hearty ranch life Roosevelt enjoyed in the Badlands turned out to be just what he needed. Every morning he rose before dawn and spent hours horseback riding. The cowboys who helped take care of his herd were impressed, but because he wore glasses, they sometimes called him Four-Eyes behind his back. Once they broke into loud laughter when Roosevelt urged a cowboy who was looking for some stray calves to "hasten forward quickly there." Why didn't he simply say, "Hurry up?" they wondered. But Roosevelt, for all his frail appearance and fancy language worked as hard as the sturdiest cowboy.

During his time in the Badlands, Roosevelt lived the life of a cowboy. He fought prairie fires and once spent an entire night chasing stampeding cattle.

Roosevelt still grieved for his wife and mother. At moments, he felt he had nothing to live for. But slowly, his spirit began to heal just as his body began to toughen. Even his voice became more powerful. In the face of tremendous challenges, Roosevelt forged a self-confidence to match his new physical strength.

ROMANCE REKINDLED
As much as he loved the Badlands, Roosevelt had strong ties pulling him back to the East. He completed his second book, *Hunting Trips of a Ranchman,* during a long New York vacation over the winter of 1884–1885. By that summer, the new home he and Alice had planned at Oyster Bay was

Sagamore Hill, Roosevelt's home at Oyster Bay, New York

———————— ◇ ————————

finished. He named the great sprawling structure Sagamore
Hill after a Native American chief. His daughter—Baby Lee
as he called her because he still couldn't bear to say her real
name of Alice—was just learning to walk. Theodore enjoyed
playing with her on the lawn. Sometimes he also played with
his brother's daughter, little Eleanor Roosevelt.

That October, Roosevelt visited his family again after
attending the New York State Republican Convention.
One day, as he opened the door to Bamie's house, he
spied his childhood friend Edith Carow coming down
the stairs. Roosevelt froze. In the twenty months since
Alice's death, he had felt awkward about seeing Edith.

But when they began to talk, he found her company as enjoyable as ever.

After that first meeting, Roosevelt wanted to see Edith as often as he possibly could. He began calling on her and taking her to social events. Roosevelt feared that his growing attachment to Edith somehow betrayed Alice's memory. But his feelings proved too strong to resist. Before the winter was over, he asked Edith to marry him. Edith, who had always loved Roosevelt, agreed. Despite their eagerness, however, the couple felt it was too soon for him to remarry.

For the time being, they would keep their engagement a secret. Roosevelt continued to see Edith until March, when he headed west to check on his ranches. Edith set off for Europe with her mother and sister.

─────────── ✧

Edith Carow

PURSUING JUSTICE

Not long after Roosevelt returned to the Badlands, his riverboat was stolen. With two of his ranch managers, he followed the thieves in a hastily built vessel. The men had traveled along the Little Missouri River for three days and about a hundred miles when they discovered the stolen boat onshore and took the thieves by surprise. Then, prisoners in tow, Roosevelt and his men continued down the ice-jammed river.

Any hard feelings soon evaporated as Roosevelt talked and laughed with the captives. Despite freezing temperatures, he also managed to read the lengthy Russian masterpiece *Anna Karenina* before coming to shore and hiring a wagon with driver. Roosevelt loaded the prisoners onto the wagon for the inland trip to the sheriff. Hoisting his rifle, Roosevelt tramped behind the wagon for forty-five miles. That way he could make certain that no one escaped. The doctor who treated Roosevelt's sore feet called him "the most peculiar and at the same time the most wonderful man [he] had ever come to know."

BIG THINGS

Theodore was becoming well known in the Badlands. That Fourth of July, he was "orator of the day" in the town of Dickinson. "Like all Americans, I like big things," Theodore declared to the crowd of townsfolk. "Big prairies, big forests and mountains, big wheat fields, railroads." But he cautioned that wealth and success meant nothing without the proper values. "It is of more importance that we should show ourselves honest, brave,

Roosevelt enjoyed the solitude of this humble cabin, which was about 10 miles from his nearest neighbors in the Badlands.

truthful, and intelligent, than that we should own all the railways and grain elevators in the world," he declared.

Two years had passed since Roosevelt had left the New York State Assembly. After his speech, he told a local newspaper editor that he felt he belonged in politics. The editor was not surprised. In fact, he even predicted that Roosevelt could become president of the United States. "If your prophecy comes true," replied Roosevelt, "I will do my part to make a good one."

Other people also seemed to think that Roosevelt belonged in public life. When he returned to the East that October, Republicans wanted him to run for mayor of New York City. Although Roosevelt knew that his chance of winning was slight against the strong Democratic candidate, he agreed to accept the nomination.

Despite his best efforts, Roosevelt did lose the election. But the energetic campaign excited him and fueled his growing feeling that his future lay in New York. The election was scarcely over when Roosevelt set sail for London to meet Edith. They were married in a quiet ceremony on December 2, 1886.

SECOND FAMILY

After a European honeymoon, the couple returned to New York in March. That summer, Roosevelt and Edith moved into Sagamore Hill. He hung up animal heads in almost every room and lined the shelves with hundreds of books. A large room on the third floor, soon designated the "gun room," became Roosevelt's retreat. Surrounded by his rifles and souvenirs of his Badlands days, he completed another book in just over three months.

By that time, little Alice was three years old. She loved to watch her father shave in the morning. And she took special delight in a piggyback ride to breakfast each morning. On September 13, 1887, Edith gave birth to a baby boy, named after his father. Alice was fascinated, and Roosevelt was thrilled. "My little brother is a howling polly parrot," Alice proclaimed. The new baby became known as Ted.

PRESERVING THE WILDERNESS

Roosevelt was busy and content, but he still longed for the rugged life. The best place to satisfy his "restless, caged wolf feeling," was the Badlands. In November, Roosevelt set off on another hunting expedition. This time he noticed some alarming changes. The grizzly bears and elk were dying out.

The beavers had dwindled in number. Creeks had dried up, and the lush blanket of prairie grass had almost vanished. For the first time, Roosevelt realized that overhunting hurts the environment. Natural resources could no longer be taken for granted. Something had to be done to protect the animals and preserve the wilderness.

When Roosevelt returned to New York, he discussed the situation with about a dozen animal lovers, including George Bird Grinnell, the editor of *Forest and Stream* magazine. The group founded the Boone and Crockett Club, named for two of Roosevelt's favorite frontiersmen, Daniel Boone and Davy Crockett. Together the members worked for laws to preserve large game animals and to protect forest wildlife. As the club's first president, Roosevelt created the Committee on Parks, which later helped establish the National Zoo in Washington, D.C. The club also worked to increase the size of Yellowstone National Park.

———————————————— ✧ ————————————————

Roosevelt increased the size of Yellowstone National Park, which is famous for its geysers and hot springs.

Roosevelt helped Republican Benjamin Harrison (left) *campaign for the 1888 presidential election. This photo was taken after Harrion's term as president.*

✧ ————————

ANOTHER CHANCE AT PUBLIC LIFE

Since losing the race for mayor, Roosevelt's political career had been stalled. It seemed like a good time to write another book. In *The Winning of the West*, Roosevelt wanted to do more than record events. He wanted to re-create the excitement of living in past eras. He wanted readers to see, hear, and smell what it was like to travel west in a covered wagon. Roosevelt planned a multivolume work that would rank among the master-pieces of history. But it would be for general readers—not just scholars.

As absorbing as this was, Roosevelt took time from his book to campaign for Republican Benjamin Harrison in the 1888 presidential election. "I am as happy as a king," he wrote when his candidate won and the Republicans gained the majority (had the most members) in both the U.S. Senate and the House of Representatives. Despite a lack of opportunity, Roosevelt's political ambitions still flickered.

Then just weeks after Roosevelt finished *The Winning of the West,* President Harrison offered him the position of civil service commissioner. The new job didn't pay much and was not considered important. But it was Roosevelt's ticket back into public life. He jumped at the chance.

CHAPTER FIVE

HERO IN ACTION

Better a thousand times to err on the side of over-readiness to fight, than to err on the side of tame submission to injury, or cold-blooded indifference to the misery of the oppressed.
—Theodore Roosevelt to cadets (students) at the Naval War College in Rhode Island

As civil service commissioner, Roosevelt spent six years in Washington, D.C., working to ensure that government jobs were awarded fairly. Sometimes his investigations embarrassed government officials. In exasperation, the president once complained that Roosevelt "wanted to put an end to all the evil in the world between sunrise and sunset." No matter who complained, Roosevelt kept right on exposing dishonesty wherever he found it.

Theodore and Edith had three more children while they lived in Washington—a son named Kermit, a daughter named Ethel, then another son named Archibald. Theodore

Roosevelt (far left) *and his wife,* Edith (second from right),
with their children (from left to right), *Archibald,
Theodore Jr., Alice, Kermit, and Ethel*

✦

loved to listen to their adventures and join their games. In
fact, a part of him never grew up. Humorously, Edith
labeled him her "oldest and rather worst child."

A STRONGER POLICE FORCE

In 1895 Roosevelt was offered a place on New York City's
Board of Police Commissioners. His first day on the job,
Roosevelt raced up the stairs, letting his excitement spill
over into questions. "Where are our offices? Where is the
board room? What do we do first?" he exclaimed. Almost
immediately, he was elected president of the board.

There was no stopping Roosevelt once he decided what
needed to be done on the police force. Disguised in a black
cape, his face shadowed by a hat, he roamed the streets at
night checking up on the evening patrolmen. Those found

Roosevelt (second from left) *attends a meeting as president of New York City's Board of Police Commissioners.*

sleeping or neglecting their duty were summoned to his office the next day. During his two years on the police board, Roosevelt raised job standards, began photographing and fingerprinting suspects, and hired more women for office work. He had a telephone system installed so that the department could be notified of crimes more easily, and he made sure all his employees had the same high-quality weapons. Inspired by the growing popularity of bicycles, the commissioners decided to purchase some for the force. Bicycles gave policemen a big advantage when chasing criminals. The new bicycle squad made more than a thousand arrests in a single year.

THE NAVY AT LAST

Although his responsibilities were firmly fixed on New York, Roosevelt was fascinated by national events. He wanted to end European influence in North, South, and

Central Ameria—even at the cost of war. He felt Europe had no business bullying any struggling countries in South America or trying to control U.S. affairs. Roosevelt also believed the United States needed a strong navy to protect its interests and to command world respect. After William McKinley received the Republican nomination for president in 1896, Roosevelt confided to a friend, "I should like to be assistant secretary of the navy."

Roosevelt's reputation for arguing almost lost him the position. He had to wait five months after McKinley's election before his friends convinced the president that Roosevelt was the man for the job. Overflowing with ideas, Roosevelt moved back to Washington, D.C., and launched into his new responsibilities. He never tired of inspecting ships, asking questions, or suggesting new ideas. Experimental submarines and the idea of flying machines fascinated him.

One situation that particularly concerned Roosevelt was Cuba's rebellion against Spain. Cuba is an island in the Caribbean Sea, about 90 miles south of Florida. Like many Americans, Roosevelt sympathized deeply with the Cubans. Spain ruled its colony harshly. The Cubans had little self-government or freedom. If Spain's treatment of its colony got any worse, the United States might even have to aid the small island country in its fight for independence. In that case, Roosevelt told President McKinley, he would leave his government position and join the army.

Usually, Roosevelt shared important decisions with Edith. In many ways, her quiet, practical habits were a needed check to Roosevelt's spirited, sometimes rash ways. "Every morning Edie puts twenty dollars in my pocket," Roosevelt once admitted to a friend, "and to save my life I never can tell her afterward what I did with it." Edith was also the one who kept the children in line.

On November 9, 1897, Roosevelt dashed down the street on his bicycle to summon a doctor and nurse. Shortly after their arrival, Edith gave birth to her fifth child, a little boy named Quentin.

Personally and professionally, this was a demanding time for Roosevelt. Early in January, Edith came down with a lingering illness. She was still sick on January 24, when the U.S. battleship *Maine* went to Cuba. The ship's arrival was called a "courtesy visit," but its real purpose was to keep the United States informed of what was happening between the Spanish and the Cubans. Three weeks later, a tremendous explosion rocked the vessel and filled the air with smoke. The heavily damaged front portion of the ship began to sink. The explosion killed 266 men.

——————————— ✧ ———————————

Many Americans blamed Spain for the attack on the U.S.S. Maine.

Although the cause of the blast was unknown, many Americans blamed Spain and loudly called for war. Officially, Roosevelt had to remain neutral, but he spoke freely with his friends. "I would give anything if President McKinley would order the fleet to Havana [the capital of Cuba] tomorrow," he declared.

A BULL IN A CHINA SHOP

Between work and home, Roosevelt was continually trading one crisis for another. Edith's health was worsening, and his son Ted was experiencing terrible headaches. Roosevelt could think of nothing but his family problems and military plans. As far as he was concerned, the country's honor demanded revenge for the *Maine*. One Friday afternoon, his boss, U.S. Navy secretary John Long, decided to leave the office early, putting Roosevelt in charge. In a few hours, Roosevelt did everything in his power to prepare for war. He ordered coal and ammunition and relocated warships. Members of Congress received letters asking them to approve increased enlistments in the military. He even cabled Admiral George Dewey, commander of U.S. squadrons in the Far East, telling him exactly what to do in the event of war.

When Secretary John Long returned to work the next day, he was astonished. Generally a mild man, Long roared that Roosevelt had "gone at things like a bull in a china shop." But he didn't revoke a single order that Roosevelt had issued.

While the nation hovered between war and peace, Edith's life also hung in the balance. Diagnosed with a tumor in her digestive system, she underwent critical surgery. More than two weeks passed before Roosevelt was able to write, "She is crawling back to life."

TO WAR

In April 1898, Congress declared war on Spain. With Edith recovering and Ted improving, Roosevelt was determined to fight. But he was honest enough to admit afterward that nothing—not even his wife's health—could have stopped him. After he had pushed so hard for war, he felt it would have been wrong for him not to fight himself. But there may have been another reason why Roosevelt was so desperate to do battle. He had always felt uncomfortable about his father hiring a substitute to take his place during the Civil War. Fighting may have been a way to make up for his father's single flaw.

On May 6, 1898, Roosevelt left his position with the navy. He was grateful when the secretary of war gave him the chance to lead a volunteer regiment. Nevertheless, Roosevelt felt he lacked the military experience to be a commander. Instead, he accepted the position of lieutenant colonel under his friend Leonard Wood. Together they would raise a regiment to go to Cuba.

Cowboys and ranchers, policemen, musicians, and wealthy athletes all responded to Roosevelt's call for volunteers. They went to San Antonio, Texas, for training. Known as the Rough Riders, the men wore blue polka-dot handkerchiefs around their necks, and most wore sombreros (wide-brimmed hats) instead of army hats. Roosevelt was proud of their courage and determination. "In all the world there is not a regiment I would so soon belong to," he wrote to President McKinley.

Roosevelt (left) *and his friend Wood* (right) *worked together to lead a group of volunteer soldiers in the Spanish-American War* (1898).

◇

ROUGH RIDERS OR WEARY WALKERS?

Choppy seas made the landing dangerous when the Rough Riders arrived in Cuba on June 22, 1898. The men jumped from the ship into small boats pitching violently on the waves. A difficult situation got even worse when the regiment's ship slipped away with much of the soldiers' equipment still on board. All Roosevelt managed to bring ashore was a yellow raincoat, a toothbrush, and a dozen pairs of glasses sewed into his uniform and the lining of his hat.

The next afternoon, General Joseph Wheeler, commander of the cavalry division (soldiers on horseback), ordered the Rough Riders to march through the jungle to Las Guasimas,

Roosevelt (center) *was proud of the Rough Riders, who suffered heavy losses in the siege of San Juan Hill in July 1898.*

an inland mountain pass held by the enemy. Dripping with sweat and pestered by swarms of flies and gnats, the regiment trudged between masses of thick tropical vegetation. Many began to discard blankets, ponchos, coats, even cans of meat. Someone decided that "Wood's Weary Walkers" described them better than the name Rough Riders.

After more than a day of rough marching, the men heard gunfire ring out. They forced their way into thick underbrush for cover. Crawling forward, they finally came to an opening that looked across the valley. Immediately, Roosevelt ordered his men to fire at the Spanish soldiers barely visible on the opposite ridge. In desperate spurts, they advanced across the clearing, throwing themselves down in the tall grass to fire their rifles.

As days passed, Roosevelt gained experience as well as the confidence of his men. When two generals became ill with fever, his friend Wood took over one of the sick general's brigades. Roosevelt was promoted to full colonel and became the leader of the Rough Riders.

"THE GREAT DAY OF MY LIFE"
Several days later, in one-hundred-degree weather, Roosevelt led the troops along the trail toward two important ridges. San Juan Hill and Kettle Hill, teeming with enemy soldiers, blocked the way to the capital city

————————————— ✦ —————— ————

The Rough Riders charge up San Juan Hill to attack the Spanish forces in this painting from 1898.

of Santiago. These positions would have to be captured for the Americans to take the island.

As the soldiers approached San Juan Creek on July 1, a sudden storm of gunfire shattered the air. Thousands of bullets whizzed by. The water ran purple from all the blood.

Roosevelt rode up and down the ranks, rallying his troops. "Are you afraid to stand up when I am on horseback?" he challenged one soldier. A hail of bullets whistled overhead, toppling soldier after soldier. A bullet skimmed Roosevelt's elbow. "No one who saw Roosevelt take that ride expected that he would finish it alive," wrote one news reporter. Finally, at a barbed wire fence, Roosevelt was forced to dismount and proceed up the hill on foot. As the fierce troops continued their climb, the Spanish withdrew, leaving Kettle Hill to the Americans.

But the struggle continued on nearby San Juan Hill. Scrambling over rolls of wire, Roosevelt ran to join the fight. In his haste, he forgot to give orders and found that only five men had joined him. Three of them were shot as Roosevelt raced back to rouse the rest of the unit. This time all the Rough Riders braved the enemy fire to follow him down Kettle Hill, then up the side of San Juan Hill.

Other regiments were also storming the summit. Finally, the sheer number of Americans forced the Spanish to flee. Arriving at the top, Roosevelt found trenches overflowing with dead Spanish soldiers. It was important to Roosevelt to be tested in battle, and he gloried in the victory. Later, he called it, "the great day of my life."

AN HONOR LONG OVERDUE

Roosevelt felt his service in the Spanish-American War deserved a Congressional Medal of Honor. However, many military people were angry with Roosevelt. They resented the letter he had written to the War Department, telling officials what they should do. To his disappointment, Roosevelt didn't receive the medal after all. More than one hundred years later, on January 16, 2001, Congress sided with Roosevelt and honored his memory by awarding the medal.

More than one hundred years after his death, Roosevelt was awarded a Congressional Medal of Honor (right) for his bravery in the Spanish-American War.

FIGHTING DISEASE

Within days, the Spanish-American War ended with the United States' destruction of the Spanish fleet outside Santiago Harbor. But Roosevelt estimated that more than half of the Rough Riders were "dead or disabled by wounds and sickness." He fought as hard for his men as he had against the enemy, marching for miles to get them food and medicine. He also spent much of his own money on supplies.

Every day more men fell ill from yellow fever, a sometimes fatal tropical disease that is spread by mosquitoes. Roosevelt realized that his troops needed to leave the humid island, which was swarming with insects. "This army must be moved at once or perish," he wrote in a letter to the top general. All the division commanders signed it. Another letter that Roosevelt alone signed was even more strongly worded.

Somehow, news reporters got hold of both letters, and they were widely published. Officials in Washington, including the president, were furious. They had already planned to bring the troops home and were embarrassed by Roosevelt's statements. Besides, they didn't feel a volunteer should be telling them how to run the army. But to most people, Roosevelt was a hero. Even before the troops left Cuba, New York Republicans talked of nominating him for the governor of the state.

On August 15, 1898, the Rough Riders finally arrived at Montauk Point, New York. "Roosevelt! Roosevelt!" called the crowd as the troopship pulled into the dock. "Hurrah for Teddy and the Rough-Riders!"

Roosevelt's pistol bumped against his side as he raced down the gangway. "Oh, but we had a bully fight!" he declared.

CHAPTER SIX

ACCEPTANCE HAT

I have worked hard all my life, and never been particularly lucky, but this summer I was lucky, and am enjoying it to the full.

—Theodore Roosevelt to his friend,
Cecil Spring Rice

"Will you be our next governor?" someone asked Roosevelt as he stood on the dock.

"None of that," replied Roosevelt. "All I'll talk about is the regiment. It's the finest regiment there ever was, and I'm proud to command it."

The party leaders wanted Roosevelt to run, however. Who better to ensure a Republican victory than a colorful war hero? Thanks to his military victory and the resulting publicity, Roosevelt was probably the most popular man in the United States.

Shortly after leaving the army, Roosevelt met with Thomas Platt, a U.S. senator from New York, to talk about

Republican "boss" Thomas Platt was very influential in New York politics in the late 1800s.

✧ ——————————

the governorship. Platt was the most important Republican boss in New York. That meant he was the most powerful member of a small group of men who controlled politics behind the scenes. To an outsider, the political process looked simple. Republicans all over the state would choose people, called delegates, from their districts to attend the state convention. These delegates would choose, or nominate, a candidate to run against the Democratic nominee for governor. But Boss Platt had connections all over the state. Of the 971 delegates who would attend the 1898 Republican State Convention, 700 of them would vote the way Platt wanted them to. Roosevelt didn't like the idea of working with a party boss, but he knew he had no chance of becoming governor without Platt's help.

ON THE CAMPAIGN TRAIL
After the Republican delegates chose Roosevelt as their candidate, he faced a close race against his Democratic opponent, Judge Augustus Van Wyck. Roosevelt gathered

a few Rough Riders to campaign with him as he criss-crossed the state by train. Even when he gave twenty speeches in a single day, his energy didn't fade. Often he had to yell to be heard above the whistles, fireworks, and brass bands that greeted him. At a shoe factory, the employees welcomed him by cheerfully banging together the soles of the boots they were making. No wonder Roosevelt finally lost his voice.

————————— ✧ —————————

Roosevelt held the attention of crowds with his lively speeches.

But Roosevelt's very presence was more important than anything he or his fellow soldiers said. "I want to talk to you about my Colonel," said Rough Rider Buck Taylor. "He kept every promise he made to us and he will to you.... When it came to the great day he led us up San Juan Hill like sheep to the slaughter and so will he lead you."

No one seemed alarmed by such a prediction. In fact, the crowd reacted with enthusiasm. As Roosevelt's train left the station, throngs of people often surged behind, straining for one last glimpse of their hero. In November Roosevelt squeezed out a narrow victory over Van Wyck.

DEALING WITH THE "BOSS"

Roosevelt knew he would have to walk a fine line as governor. On the one hand, he had to get along with Boss Platt. On the other, he was determined to be his own man. One of Roosevelt's first challenges came when he refused to automatically appoint a man chosen by Platt as the new superintendent of public works. To Roosevelt's dismay, however, no one that he asked would accept the appointment. All the qualified candidates were afraid to go against Platt's choice. Finally, Roosevelt came up with a plan. He gave a list of four men to Platt and let him make the decision. After that, Roosevelt had frequent breakfast meetings with Platt. Roosevelt spent them trying to get Platt to accept things Roosevelt was resolved to do whether Platt liked them or not.

More than past governors, Roosevelt realized the importance of publicity. He held two press conferences each day. Seated informally on his desktop, Roosevelt told reporters all about the daily happenings. He gossiped, joked, and

Roosevelt lived in the governor's mansion in
Albany, New York, during his term as governor.

─────────── ✧ ───────────

shared stories. The reporters scarcely had time to ask their own questions, but they had plenty of news to cover.

Roosevelt's efforts led to the passage of many reform bills—including measures to protect the wilderness and a ban against throwing sawdust waste from logging into mountain streams. He worked to get higher pay for teachers and to prevent local school districts from practicing racial segregation. "My children sit in the same school with [African American] children," he said to emphasize his feelings on the matter.

Improving conditions in sweatshops also claimed a great deal of Roosevelt's attention. Sweatshops were crowded, unhealthy factories where women and children labored many hours each day. Roosevelt championed and signed bills to protect factory workers, to limit state employees to an eight-hour day, and to restrict the hours women and children had to work.

Taxes were another important issue. Most New Yorkers paid high taxes. Roosevelt felt strongly that big business should pay its fair share of taxes too. Boss Platt, who relied on support from big business, was furious. But Roosevelt did everything in his power to strengthen the tax reform bill and see that it passed. When he finally signed the bill, he called it "the most important law passed in recent times by any State Legislature." Boss

————————————— ✧ —————————————

Many poor immigrant children were forced to work in sweatshops in the early 1900s. These young women participate in a demonstration in New York City.

Platt, however, began to think that it had been a mistake to support Roosevelt for governor.

NEVER AN IDLE MOMENT
After his tax reform victory, Roosevelt felt that he'd earned a little time off. In June 1899, he took off for a reunion of the Rough Riders in New Mexico. July found him back at Sagamore Hill with his family. "I don't mean to do one single thing during this month," he told his sister, "except write a life of Oliver Cromwell [a famous British statesman]."

Writing a biography in a month's time is a huge job. But Roosevelt didn't waste a minute. Every morning he looked over his notes and several reference books. Then he had a secretary write down his words as he talked almost nonstop. Sometimes he had two secretaries. Turning to one, he would compose a paragraph of his book. Turning to the other, he would recite a paragraph for an official letter. Back and forth he went, never losing his train of thought. Often a barber shaved him at the same time.

SPEAK SOFTLY AND CARRY A BIG STICK
During his second term as governor, Roosevelt again turned his attention to large companies. He thought they should tell the public how much money they made and then pay a fair amount of taxes. Boss Platt was losing all patience with Roosevelt. Relations between the two men became even worse when Roosevelt refused to reappoint a dishonest official who was one of Platt's loyal followers.

Quietly, Roosevelt held his ground until Platt gave in. The governor used an old African proverb, or saying, to sum up his policy. "Speak softly and carry a big stick; you

Roosevelt (center) was prepared to back up his words with action.

will go far." Roosevelt always did this. No matter how calmly he discussed an issue, he was ready to back up his words with force.

THE NEXT STEP

Boss Platt was determined to get Roosevelt out of New York politics. His plan was simple. If Roosevelt were elected vice president of the United States, Platt wouldn't have to bother with him anymore. He thought he could "bury" Roosevelt in a job that would keep him busy but give him little real power.

This was not the first time the subject of Roosevelt running for vice president had been raised. Roosevelt's friend Henry Cabot Lodge had suggested it for a different reason. He thought the vice presidency would serve as a good springboard for Roosevelt to run for president at a later date. Roosevelt disagreed. He wanted to be president someday, but he feared the vice presidency would not provide enough action for him.

As the Republican National Convention of 1900 drew near, Platt had newspapers print stories suggesting Roosevelt as the best candidate for the job. "Under no circumstances could I or would I accept the nomination for the vice presidency," Roosevelt declared. "I would a great deal rather be anything, say a professor of history, than vice president."

Despite such protests, Platt kept gathering support and even arranged for Roosevelt to be a delegate to the convention in Philadelphia, Pennsylvania. Lodge cautioned his friend that if he attended, he would definitely be chosen. Roosevelt objected that he had to attend to show once and for all that he did *not* want to be vice president.

But once he arrived in Philadelphia, Roosevelt's resolve began to weaken. He knew he could not run for governor again without Platt's backing. He also realized that tremendous support was building to include him on the Republican ticket with President William McKinley. Did he really want to stop the growing movement?

The first day of the convention, Roosevelt arrived late on purpose. He was wearing a wide-brimmed Rough Rider's hat. While the people shouted, "We want Teddy," a man in the audience turned to the people seated near him. "Gentlemen," he said, "that's an acceptance hat."

Roosevelt's powerful speaking style roused the enthusiasm of his listeners. He made thousands of speeches in his political career. Here he makes a speech at Carnegie Hall in New York City.

CHAPTER SEVEN

A BULLY PULPIT

That man in the White House is stupendous.
I went in as angry as a hornet, and
before I was through in there I was
liking him in spite of myself.
—Senator John Spooner of Wisconsin
speaking of President Roosevelt

Only one delegate didn't vote for Roosevelt's nomination as vice president. That was Roosevelt himself. Such a landslide could not be ignored. Once Roosevelt agreed to run, he could hardly wait to begin campaigning. "I am as strong as a bull moose and you can use me up to the limit," he told the chairman of the Republican Party.

By Election Day, he had made 673 speeches to about three million people and traveled over 21,000 miles. Meanwhile, McKinley conducted his campaign from his front porch. "'Tis Teddy alone that's r-runninn', and he ain't runninn', he's gallopin'," remarked a newspaper reporter.

Roosevelt (right) served as vice president with President William McKinley (left) from 1900 to 1901. Above is a campaign poster from the presidential race.

———————————— ✧ ————————————

Roosevelt's galloping paid off. On November 6, 1900, the Republicans defeated Democratic candidate William Jennings Bryan. Four months later, on March 4, 1901, Roosevelt took the vice presidential oath of office in the Senate chamber of the Capitol in Washington, D.C. In their excitement, his younger children nearly toppled over the balcony railing.

But Roosevelt didn't find his new job very exciting. For four days in March, he oversaw meetings of the Senate. Then the Senate adjourned (temporarily ended), and Roosevelt's official duties were at an end until

December. "The vice president. . . is really a fifth wheel to the coach," he observed in disappointment.

NATIONAL TRAGEDY

Roosevelt was getting ready for a reception in Vermont on September 6 when he learned that a deranged man named Leon Czolgosz had shot President McKinley. Dropping everything, Roosevelt rushed to Buffalo, New York, where the president had been attending the Pan American Exposition, a fair celebrating North and South America. One of the bullets had ripped through the president's stomach, but it seemed McKinley would survive.

Relieved, Roosevelt met his family in the Adirondack Mountains. Then came the terrible news that the president had taken a turn for the worse. Roosevelt began his desperate ride down the mountainside. By the time he arrived at the train station, McKinley had died.

─────────────── ✧ ───────────────

President William McKinley was shot by Leon Czolgosz on September 6, 1901, in Buffalo, New York.

Theodore Roosevelt was sworn in as president at the
Wilcox house in Buffalo, New York.

———————————— ✧ ————————————

"Hurrah for Teddy!" several people called when his train
arrived in Buffalo, New York. A stony-faced Roosevelt
stared them into silence. After paying his respects to
McKinley's widow, he went to a friend's house to take the
oath of office. Forty-three witnesses watched as Roosevelt
tensely raised his right hand and swore to uphold the office
of the presidency. His first official act was to declare a day
of mourning for McKinley.

AT HOME IN THE WHITE HOUSE

Roosevelt moved into the White House on September 23,
1901, his father's birthday. That meant a lot to the new

president. He felt as if his father's spirit were present, encouraging and blessing him as he began his greatest responsibility and challenge.

One of the first things Roosevelt did was invite African American educator Booker T. Washington to dinner. No other African American had ever dined in the White House. Roosevelt wanted Washington's help in identifying qualified people, both black and white, to hold government posts in the South.

To Roosevelt's surprise, a storm of protest arose in the South when people learned about the dinner. "I am very glad that I asked him," a startled Roosevelt declared, "for the clamor aroused by the act makes me feel as if the act was necessary." Although he continued to rely on Washington's advice, Roosevelt didn't invite him or any other black person to dinner again.

——————— ✧

Booker T. Washington was the first African American dinner guest at the White House.

When Roosevelt became president, he and Edith moved their family into the White House.

Visitors, especially reformers, flocked to see the new president. People were amazed by Roosevelt's energy, intelligence, and confidence. "Dee-lighted!" Roosevelt greeted his guests, though he had little time to chat. "Tell me what you have to say quickly, quickly!" he often urged.

As Roosevelt adjusted to his new responsibilities, his children made themselves at home in the White House. They rode their bicycles over the lawns and roller-skated in the basement. They clattered on their stilts through the grand public rooms. Every evening before dinner, Edith gathered them for stories. Roosevelt, who loved the stories as much as his children, often came to listen and ended up romping on the floor with them. As soon as Edith gave the word, the rowdy gang (Roosevelt included) would instantly rise to get ready for dinner.

MESSAGE TO CONGRESS

Roosevelt had always had a lot to say. And since he was president, people had to listen. Only half joking, he called the presidency a "bully pulpit," an exciting public platform, from which to proclaim his views. In December he presented his first annual message to Congress. It was the longest in the history of the presidency.

Roosevelt's message tackled many different issues. He thought there should be special laws to protect working women and children. He wanted more land set aside for forests and new projects for flood control and irrigation to be started. To keep the country strong, Roosevelt wanted more naval battleships. And he thought a canal should be

─────────── ✧

Roosevelt greets famous reformer Jane Addams, who shared many of his social concerns.

built connecting the Atlantic and Pacific oceans across the narrow strip of Central America. Ships would be able to travel from ocean to ocean without the long voyage around the tip of South America.

Roosevelt also covered the important topic of big business. As industries merged into huge companies, sometimes called trusts, smaller businesses found it hard to compete with them. Roosevelt wanted to be fair to both sides. He realized that big business wasn't always bad and could even do a lot of good.

However, big business could also drive smaller companies out of business. That meant the large companies could raise their prices. Customers had no other place to turn to for goods and services. Roosevelt was well aware of the danger. "In the interest of the public, the government should have the right to inspect and examine the workings of the great corporations [large companies]," he declared.

CONTROLLING BIG BUSINESS

By February 1902, Roosevelt was ready to act on his words. A new company called Northern Securities had been made by joining together two railroad firms. Its creation broke a law known as the Sherman Anti-Trust Act. The purpose of the law was to prevent any company from getting too large and taking too much business away from smaller firms. Although the Sherman Anti-Trust Act had never been tested, Roosevelt decided to file a lawsuit. He felt that Northern Securities did pose a threat to smaller companies. That was not in the best interest of the public either. A lawsuit would let all big businesses know that they had to obey the rules. Eventually, the suit made its way to the Supreme Court, which agreed with Roosevelt's position. Northern Securities would have to be broken up into smaller companies.

COAL CRISIS

Roosevelt's family spent the first summer of his presidency at Sagamore Hill while the White House was being remodeled. After a day spent conducting official business in the library, he might pitch in with the work on his farm or go riding or play tennis with the children. On more formal occasions when guests came to dine, the children ate with them. Contrary to the popular view that "children should be seen and not heard," Roosevelt encouraged them to talk and ask questions.

By the time the family returned to Washington in September 1902, another crisis was sending ripples of alarm throughout the country. A coal strike had begun in eastern Pennsylvania in May. Miners, some of them children, worked twelve hours each day, six days a week, in dangerous

────────────── ✧ ──────────────

These coal miners worked long hours in dangerous conditions. In 1902 they went on strike to demand better working conditions.

The shortage of coal during the coal workers strike of 1902 had people concerned for the cold winter that was fast approaching.

————————— ◇

underground conditions. They made $560 a year, but much of that went back to the company for rent, groceries, and other goods. Struggling to make ends meet, the miners found themselves constantly in debt to the company.

The managers refused to recognize the United Mine Workers organization or listen to their demands for better hours, safer working conditions, and higher salaries. As winter approached, people began to get worried. Without fuel for their furnaces, many families faced the prospect of a bitterly cold winter.

Roosevelt brought both sides together for a conference in Washington on October 3. But no agreement was reached. "Well, I have tried and failed," he said gloomily.

People around the nation were scared and angry—especially in coal country. Some gave vent to their frustrations through acts of violence. They flooded mines, blew up bridges, and caused train accidents. The weather grew worse with no relief in sight. Finally, Roosevelt threatened to send in army troops to run the mines during the crisis. Nothing in the Constitution gave Roosevelt the power to interfere in this way. But when a congressman objected, Roosevelt exclaimed, almost angrily, "The Constitution was made for the people and not the people for the Constitution."

Before Roosevelt had to act on his threat, both sides agreed to accept the rulings of a five-person commission. The miners returned to work, and the company shortened the working day by one hour and gave the men a 10 percent raise. Looking back on the coal strike, Roosevelt said that he had wanted a "square deal" for both the miners and the bosses. Later, that phrase would be applied to many programs in his presidency.

FROM SEA TO SEA

Over the next few years, Roosevelt handled some critical issues. He expanded the Monroe Doctrine, which was a statement against European interference in the Western Hemisphere. He also continued to urge the construction of a canal connecting the Atlantic and Pacific oceans across Central America.

The problem was that Panama was not an independent country. It belonged to the South American country of Colombia. The United States proposed a treaty for control of a six-mile strip of land where the canal could be built, but Colombia wanted more money. The people of Panama, however, were eager for the canal. They decided to revolt against Colombia and make their own treaty with the United States.

The United States started working on the Panama Canal in 1903.
The French had begun work on the project in the 1880s.

———————————————————— ✧ ————————————————————

In 1903 Roosevelt gave behind-the-scenes support to Panama's rebellion. When Panama quickly gained its independence, the United States began work on the canal. Meanwhile, Roosevelt also continued to expand the navy.

WATCH OUT FOR ME

In his third annual message to Congress, Roosevelt declared, "The country is to be congratulated on the amount of substantial achievement which has marked the past year as regards our foreign and as regards our domestic policy [policy relating to the United States]." But despite his proud words, Roosevelt felt nervous about the approaching presidential election. For three years, he had been an "accidental" president. Would the public vote for

him, as they had voted for President McKinley? Roosevelt
hated the uncertainty. On November 8, 1904, he cast his
vote at Oyster Bay, then returned by train to Washington.

By the time the polls closed, Roosevelt's waiting was
over. "How they are voting for me!" he declared as the
election returns came in. Roosevelt defeated his Democratic
opponent, Judge Alton Parker, by a landslide. But in his
excitement, Roosevelt made a rash statement. He said that
he would not run for president again when his term
expired. Four years seemed a long time, and he had no
inkling he might one day regret his words. The day before
his inauguration on March 4, 1904, Roosevelt declared,
"Tomorrow I shall come into my office in my own right.
Then watch out for me!"

———————————— ✧ ————————————

After winning the presidential election by two and a half million votes,
Roosevelt was inaugurated on March 4, 1905.

Scarcely had his new term begun when Roosevelt went to New York for the wedding of his niece Eleanor Roosevelt. As her closest male relative, the president gave the bride away to Franklin Delano Roosevelt, a distant cousin. Even at the wedding, Roosevelt stood out. More eyes were focused on him than on the bride!

Roosevelt's daughter Alice got married about a year later. Once again Roosevelt marched the bride down the aisle, this time in the East Room of the White House. Strong-willed and wild for the times, Alice had often been a trial to her father. Once when someone asked why he

✧ ————————————
Roosevelt (right) *with his daughter Alice* (center) *and her husband, Nicholas Longworth* (left)

didn't control his daughter better, Roosevelt replied, "I can be president of the United States or I can control Alice. I can't possibly do both." But Alice was and continued to be his most loyal supporter.

NEGOTIATING PEACE

Roosevelt exerted his authority in international affairs as well as domestic programs. He believed that the United States could not afford to be isolated from what went on in the rest of the world. The war going on between Japan and Russia concerned Americans too because it might change the relationship between nations. Japan had recently defeated Russia in a major battle. Roosevelt did not want Japan to be strong enough to threaten peace in other parts of the world. Nor did he want the Russian government to collapse.

Roosevelt persuaded both countries to send diplomats to the United States for a peace conference. On August 5, 1905, Roosevelt had lunch with the Japanese and Russian delegates on the presidential yacht near Oyster Bay. Both groups were keenly aware of their dignity and sensitive to any slights. Linking arms with the chief Japanese and chief Russian delegates, Roosevelt kept up a lively conversation so no one would notice who entered the dining room first.

After the opening lunch, the delegates left for the peace conference that was held at Portsmouth, New Hampshire. From Sagamore Hill, Roosevelt followed the negotiations closely. Finally, the delegates came to agreement, signing the peace treaty in September 1905. "It's a mighty good thing for Russia," Roosevelt declared, "and a mighty good thing

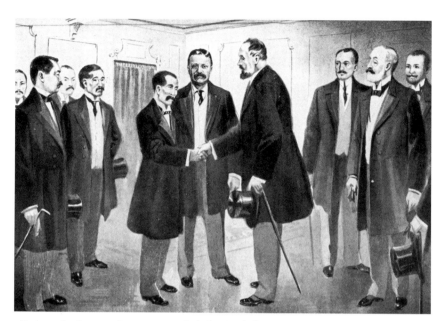

Roosevelt (center) was awarded the Nobel Peace Prize for his role in the peace talks between Japan and Russia in 1905, pictured above.

for Japan." Thumping his chest, he added, "And a mighty good thing for me, too!" The next year, Roosevelt became the first U.S. president to win the Nobel Peace Prize. This international award is given to individuals who make outstanding contributions to world peace.

SWEEPING REFORMS

Meanwhile, Roosevelt drew up a list of domestic issues to push through Congress. The annual message he sent to the nation's lawmakers on December 5, 1905, presented his vision for the future. He wanted railroad rates to be regulated and child labor to be carefully studied. He wanted the government to oversee insurance companies, and he wanted a new law passed to ensure that all food and drugs would be safe. People weren't used to the government being concerned with so many business and public safety issues.

Roosevelt got much of what he wanted. In 1906 the Hepburn Railway Rate Act was passed, giving the Interstate Commerce Commission more power to supervise railroad rates. This would prevent railway executives from giving cheaper shipping prices to large companies. Such favors made it difficult for small businesses to survive.

The nation's food supply was also in trouble. A book called *The Jungle* by a writer named Upton Sinclair had readers in an uproar. Sinclair described the disgusting and dangerous methods used in Chicago meatpacking plants. A can of beef might contain meat from sick cattle. Ground rats and even rat dung might find its way into sausage. Often no chicken was in cans that were labeled "canned chicken." The Meat Inspection Bill and the Pure Food and Drug Act made sure that canned foods would not be contaminated (made dirty) or diluted (weakened). Americans could be sure that the food they bought was safe to eat.

Conservation was another issue that Roosevelt championed energetically. During Roosevelt's administrations, 150 million acres were set aside as government land reserves. This would keep lumber companies from cutting down entire forests. Roosevelt created five national parks and more than fifty wildlife preserves. In addition, under the Preservation of American Antiquities Act of 1906, Roosevelt had the power to declare certain areas national monuments without any approval from Congress. Among the fifteen monuments he established this way were the

Grand Canyon in Arizona, Niagara Falls in New York, and the Muir Woods in California.

Even when there were no laws, Roosevelt did everything he could to save wildlife and natural resources. He was surprised to learn that the exotic birds on an island off Florida were being hunted into extinction (in danger of all dying out). "Is there any law that will prevent me from declaring Pelican Island a federal bird reserve?" he asked. "Very well, then I do so declare it."

———————————————— ✧ ————————————————

Roosevelt established wildlife refuges in seventeen states and territories, including Pelican Island off the Florida coast.

*This political cartoon pokes
fun at Roosevelt's interest
in many different things.*
——————————— ✧

A FINGER IN EVERY PIE

Roosevelt meddled in almost
everything. He called a special
meeting to help make football safer for the players. He
insisted on taking a ride in one of the navy's first
submarines. In fact, he even tried to steer it, and he did
manage to bring the vessel to the surface. The only problem
was that the back end came up first. The public respected
Roosevelt, but many people thought it was silly when he
tried to change the spelling of three hundred words.
Newspapers all over the country made fun of him.
"Nuthing escapes Mr. Rucevelt," announced a Louisville,
Kentucky, paper. "[He] will reform spelling in a way tu
soot himself." The changes never took hold.

On his trip to Panama, Roosevelt (wearing a white suit and hat,
standing in the digging machine) *visited the construction site of the
Panama Canal and tried out the steam-powered digging machine.*

In November 1906, Roosevelt became the first president
to travel to a foreign country while still in office. He and
Edith went to Panama to see the canal. Once again, like an
excited youngster, he had to try out a piece of equipment.
Stomping through the mud, he climbed into a giant steam
shovel while a photographer snapped his photo. Although
progress on the canal was slower than he would have liked,
Roosevelt had nothing but praise for the work crews.

AROUND THE WORLD

While Roosevelt explored Panama, another crisis with Japan
loomed on the horizon. One month earlier, in October
1906, the school board of the city of San Francisco had
placed all Japanese children in their own separate school.

The Japanese people were outraged. Anti-American protests broke out all over Japan. Roosevelt too was angry. He promised a Japanese friend that he would use "all the power I have under the Constitution to protect the rights of the Japanese people who are here."

But in May of 1907, people publicly protested the growing number of immigrants in San Francisco. Roosevelt feared possible war with Japan. As a show of American might, he decided to send sixteen battleships on a world-wide tour. Never had so many ships sailed so far together. On December 16, 1907, the Great White Fleet, as the ships were called, began its voyage from Hampton Roads, Virginia. From the deck of the presidential yacht, Roosevelt waved his top hat and watched as each ship cruised past. "By George, isn't it magnificent!" he exclaimed.

───────────────── ✧ ─────────────────

Roosevelt displayed the power of the United States to the world with the tour of sixteen U.S. battleships called the Great White Fleet.

All over the world, people jammed the harbors to glimpse the great ships and the sailors. Even the streets of Yokohama, Japan, were lined with children waving small U.S. flags as the sailors left ship and marched past. The visit, intended as a show of American might, also led to an increase of goodwill between the United States and Japan.

By the time the fleet returned home on February 22, 1909, Roosevelt's term of office was almost over. The Republicans had won the presidential election of 1908. True to his word, Roosevelt had declined to run again. But knowing his support would be important, he had picked the man he wanted to run in his place—William Howard Taft. It was snowing when the Tafts arrived at the White House the day before the inauguration. "I knew there'd be a blizzard when I went out!" joked Roosevelt.

A Very Famous Bear

Even as president, Roosevelt took time for what he called "the strenuous life." In 1902 Roosevelt went bear hunting in Mississippi. After five days without spotting an animal, he received word that his hunting partners had tracked one down. Roosevelt raced ten miles to the scene to discover a small, frightened bear covered with blood and mud. He refused to shoot the defenseless creature.

Word of Roosevelt's sense of fair play leaked out. A Washington cartoonist, Clifford Berryman, commemorated the event with a humorous drawing. The public loved it. More bear cartoons followed, each one more appealing than the last. Soon the toy industry got into the act. A businessman made several small stuffed bears to sell in his Brooklyn toy store. According to tradition, he wrote a letter asking if he could name his new creation after the president. "I don't think my name will mean much to the bear business," replied Roosevelt. But, in this case, Roosevelt was wrong! Soon children all over the country were clamoring for teddy bears *(right)*.

Roosevelt (right) and his son Kermit (left) took four tons of salt on safari in Africa in 1909 to preserve the skins of all the animals they expected to kill. The men are pictured here with a water buffalo.

CHAPTER EIGHT

A PROMISE KEPT

I know no other man who has had as good
a time as I have had in life; no other
President ever enjoyed the Presidency as I did;
no other ex-President ever enjoyed himself
as I am now enjoying myself.

—Theodore Roosevelt, writing from Africa
to his friend Henry Cabot Lodge

The retiring president was barely fifty years old. Despite his determination to avoid a third term, it was hard for him to leave office. For nearly eight years, he had thrived on the power, the tension, and the responsibility of the presidency. Roosevelt knew he had to plan something to keep from feeling let down when he left Washington. When he left office in March 1909, he chose the greatest adventure he could think of—a year hunting big game in Africa. Since Roosevelt didn't want to kill animals simply for the sake of killing, he made arrangements to donate all his specimens to the Smithsonian Institution and other museums. By the time the safari was over, Roosevelt had killed nine lions, seven giraffes, twenty zebras, seven hippopotamuses, eight elephants, and three pythons.

Soon Roosevelt joined his wife and daughter in Egypt. Following a trip down the Nile River, they began a tour of Europe. Wherever Roosevelt went, world leaders extended invitations and common folks flocked to hear him speak. In Christiania (renamed Oslo in 1925), Norway, he finally gave his acceptance speech for the Nobel Peace Prize. Roosevelt spoke of the need for an international organization to enforce peace. He called it a League of Peace and said it should use force, if necessary, to stop nations from waging war. Later, people would remember Roosevelt's words. At the time, a London newspaper called his idea "too fantastic to be realized."

HOMECOMING

A great celebration awaited Theodore and Edith when they arrived in New York on June 18, 1910. After attending their son Ted's wedding, they looked forward to some much-needed relaxation at Sagamore Hill. But it seemed impossible for Roosevelt ever to live a quiet life. Within weeks of his homecoming, he was on the road again, giving speeches throughout the Midwest. It didn't matter where he spoke—whether in a state legislature or a baseball stadium—crowds rallied to his cries for reform.

Roosevelt's demands for social justice went far beyond the views of his successor, President Taft. Roosevelt was also unhappy because he felt that Taft didn't do enough about conservation. Many people shared his views and missed his

"IS THAT THE BEST CARE YOU COULD TAKE OF MY CAT?"

Roosevelt (right) *felt that President Taft* (left) *neglected the policies (represented in this cartoon as a skinny cat) that he had worked so hard to create.*

forceful presence in government. They urged him to run again for the presidency in 1912. Although it meant opposing his former friend Taft, Roosevelt couldn't resist. "My hat is in the ring!" he announced.

THE BULL MOOSE

Roosevelt's chances of winning the Republican nomination looked good. He won 278 delegates in the state primaries—far more than Taft. If all these delegates had voted for Roosevelt at the Republican convention, he would have become the party candidate easily. But some party members were determined to see Taft reelected. They raised objections to Roosevelt's delegates and supported delegates of their own. Which group of delegates had been selected legally? The Republican choice for president depended on the answer to that question.

Tensions ran high as the roll call vote drew near. In the end, the Republican National Committee awarded most of the questionable delegate seats to Taft's people. Despite Roosevelt's popular support, President Taft was chosen as the Republican candidate.

But the excitement started by Roosevelt's reentry into politics could not be stopped. His supporters marched angrily out of the convention hall in Chicago. It took them only seven weeks to organize a new political party, the Progressives (nicknamed the Bull Moose Party) and to nominate Roosevelt as their candidate for president.

◇ ————————

Roosevelt campaigned as the Bull Moose Party's presidential candidate in 1912.

Roosevelt threw himself into the campaign like the veteran fighter he was. Even with the Republican Party split, Roosevelt knew he might defeat Taft. However, his chances for victory were slight against Democrat Woodrow Wilson. That didn't stop him from visiting cities all over the country. On October 14, 1912, in Milwaukee, Wisconsin, Roosevelt was standing before a throng of people when a man pulled out a gun and shot him at close range.

"I don't know whether you fully understand that I have just been shot," he declared moments later at a rally, "but it takes more than that to kill a bull moose." He pulled a copy of his speech from his jacket to show off the bullet hole. A metal eyeglass case and the bulky pages of his speech had slowed down the bullet and saved his life. "The bullet is in me now," Roosevelt continued, "so that I cannot make a very long speech but I will try my best." He spoke for an hour and a half before his anxious aides could persuade him to go to the hospital.

THE CALL OF THE JUNGLE

Although Roosevelt wasn't seriously injured, he couldn't campaign again before Election Day. He was not surprised when Democratic candidate Woodrow Wilson won the presidency. Roosevelt needed something new to take his mind off his failed attempt to recapture the White House. He decided to write his autobiography, emphasizing some of his most exciting experiences, such as hunting in the Badlands and breaking up the coal strike.

When he was done writing, Roosevelt grew restless for more adventure. Soon he was planning an exploring trip through the Amazon region of Brazil in South America.

"I have to go," he explained happily. "It's my last chance to be a boy!"

Kermit joined his father on a dangerous journey to explore the course of the River of Doubt. With their companions and guides, they chopped their way through thick growth. Dangerous rapids hindered their passage on the river. Trying to save two wildly bobbing canoes, Roosevelt injured his leg badly. A serious infection set in.

As supplies ran low, he worried that the others wouldn't make it back if they had to care for him. He begged to be left alone to die. Kermit wouldn't hear of it. When the weary travelers finally reached a village, Roosevelt had lost fifty-seven pounds. Still unsteady on his feet, he arrived in New York in May 1914. Waving his cane, he called playfully to reporters, "You see I still have the big stick."

DECLARATION OF WAR

If Roosevelt had still been president, he probably would have shaken that famous "stick" after World War I broke out in Europe in 1914. He felt certain that Germany was a growing threat and that the United States should strengthen its army and navy. But President Wilson and his secretary of state, William Jennings Bryan, didn't see any need to build up military forces. Their attitude angered Roosevelt.

Like most other Americans, Roosevelt was stunned to learned that a German submarine had torpedoed and sunk the British passenger ship S.S. *Lusitania* on May 7, 1915. When Roosevelt learned that almost 1,200 people had died, including 128 U.S. citizens, he was outraged. "That's murder!" he yelled. "It is warfare against innocent men, women, and children."

More than one hundred U.S. citizens were killed when the Lusitania (above) was torpedoed by a German submarine in 1915.

For almost two years, Roosevelt remained angry. Justice demanded that some action be taken against Germany. But Wilson wasn't ready for strong measures. "Lord, how I would like to be president!" Roosevelt confided to a friend.

Some Republicans liked that idea too. They wanted him to return to their party and run against Wilson. Roosevelt felt a small surge of hope as more and more Republicans began to support him. However, he still had powerful enemies, angry at his leaving the party four years earlier. They controlled the convention and refused to even let him speak. Once again, Roosevelt lost the Republican nomination. And once again, the Progressives chose him as their candidate. But this time, he did not heed the call. He knew that the Progressive Party was not strong enough to win the election and refused the nomination. Wilson was reelected.

In January 1917, Germany announced its intent to open submarine warfare on all ships in the waters near its enemies. Forced to act at last, Wilson broke off official communications between the two countries. The German ambassador in Washington returned home, and the U.S. ambassador in Germany left. Soon German submarines sank three U.S. merchant (commercial) ships. The entire mood of the country changed. In early April, Wilson asked Congress to declare war on Germany.

ONE MORE CHANCE?

Shortly after the United States entered the war, Roosevelt went to see Wilson at the White House. It couldn't have been easy to visit the man he had criticized so often, but Roosevelt had a big favor to ask. At first the president greeted his critic stiffly. But Roosevelt's humor and warmth soon softened Wilson up. The men chatted and laughed like old friends.

Roosevelt desperately wanted to fight. He wanted permission to raise and lead a special regiment just as he had years earlier in the Spanish-American War. He hoped his deeds—and perhaps even his death—would honor his family name. In the end, however, Wilson decided not to let him raise a volunteer regiment. Deeply disappointed, Roosevelt watched his four adult sons go to war instead. "It's rather up to us to practice what Father preaches," said Quentin, who became a fighter pilot.

Roosevelt's youngest son, Quentin (right), *was a fighter pilot in World War I.*

Meanwhile, Roosevelt busied himself on the home front. He wrote articles and traveled from city to city, promoting the Red Cross and urging people to buy Liberty Bonds. The money the government made from the sale of the bonds supported the war effort. When his son Archie complained of a shortage of shoes among his men, Roosevelt paid for six hundred pairs. He also provided food, blankets, and arms.

By this time, Theodore Roosevelt had eight grandchildren, who helped take his mind off the dangers his sons faced. He had wanted his sons to fight and had helped them to get good positions. But sometimes he woke up in the middle of the night, sick with worry.

In July 1918, Theodore and Edith received word that Quentin's plane had been shot down over France. Quentin was dead. The grief-stricken parents kept up a show of courage in public, but their sorrow was almost unbearable.

Hoping to escape the press, they retreated to an island off the coast of Maine. Theodore spent hours staring sorrowfully at the ocean.

A PROMISE KEPT

Sixty-year-old Roosevelt was not in good health. He suffered from rheumatism, which caused pain in his muscles and joints, and a disease called gout, which caused his ankles to swell painfully. Gritting his teeth, Roosevelt limped a mile to the polls on Election Day. He said that if he couldn't fight, voting was the least he could do for his country. Shortly afterward, on November 11, 1918, Germany surrendered.

That same day, Roosevelt entered the hospital with fever, a blood disease, and dizziness. "Well, no matter what comes," he told his sister Corinne Robinson, "I have kept the promise I made to myself when I was twenty-one."

"What was that?" asked Corinne.

Roosevelt still had the energy to pound his fist for emphasis. "I promised myself that I would work up to the hilt until I was sixty, and I have done it."

THE OLD LION

On Christmas Day 1918, Theodore was released from the hospital. Surrounded by his family, he enjoyed a quiet holiday. Over the next few days, he regained strength and began writing again. Just before going to bed on January 5, he told Edith, "I wonder if you will ever know how I love Sagamore Hill." That night Theodore died in his sleep. Archie, home from the war, cabled his brothers, "The old lion is dead."

LARGER THAN LIFE

Sculptor Gutzon Borglum was a friend of Roosevelt and campaigned vigorously for him in the election of 1912. Years later, when he was designing his famous monument on Mount Rushmore, in South Dakota, he wanted to include Roosevelt. Some people said that Roosevelt was too recent a figure to include with Washington, Jefferson, and Lincoln. Borglum felt that Roosevelt had done so much for the working man that no honor was too great for his friend and his hero. In 1939, twenty-one years after Roosevelt's death, the enormous granite sculpture of the president's face was unveiled.·

---◇---

Mount Rushmore is located in South Dakota's Black Hills. The sculptures (from left to right), are of Washington, Jefferson, Roosevelt, and Lincoln.

Five hundred people jammed into the small church at Oyster Bay for the funeral. A New York policeman turned to Corinne. "Do you remember the fun of him, Mrs. Robinson?" he asked with tears in his eyes.

For years Theodore Roosevelt had bulldozed his way through history, willing to risk everything on what he thought was right. In his own words, "I did and caused to be done many things not previously done by the president and heads of the departments. In other words, I acted for the public welfare." By following his beliefs, he made the presidency a more powerful office, brought about a

———————— ✧ ————————

Roosevelt is remembered as an energetic president who worked hard to improve life for the American people.

stronger government, and increased U.S. involvement in foreign affairs.

People might disagree with Roosevelt's decisions, but no one could doubt his courage or patriotism. Vice President Thomas Marshall summed up the feelings of many Americans when he declared, "Death had to take him sleeping, for if Roosevelt had been awake there would have been a fight."

TIMELINE

1858   Theodore Roosevelt is born on October 27.

1880   Roosevelt graduates from Harvard. He marries Alice Lee on his twenty-second birthday.

1881   Roosevelt is elected to the New York State legislature.

1882   Roosevelt's first book, *The Naval War of 1812*, is published.

1883   Roosevelt buys a ranch in the Dakota Badlands.

1884   Daughter Alice is born February 12. His wife and mother die February 14.

1886   Roosevelt marries Edith Carow on December 2.

1887   His son Theodore Jr. is born.

1889   Roosevelt becomes a civil service commissioner. *The Winning of the West*, Volume 1, is published.

1890   Son Kermit is born.

1891   Daughter Ethel is born.

1894   Son Archie is born.

1895   Roosevelt becomes head of the New York police board.

1897   Roosevelt becomes assistant secretary of the navy. Son Quentin is born.

1898   Roosevelt leads the Rough Riders' charge up San Juan Hill in the Spanish-American War. He is elected governor of New York.

1900   Roosevelt is elected vice president.

1901   Roosevelt becomes president after the assassination of William McKinley. Roosevelt invites Booker T. Washington to dinner, the first time an African American had been asked to dine at the White House.

1902 Roosevelt uses the Sherman Anti-Trust Act against big business. He forces settlement of a coal strike that threatens public welfare.

1903 Roosevelt quietly provides U.S. support for Panama's rebellion against Colombia to set up U.S. involvement in the construction of the Panama Canal.

1904 Roosevelt is reelected president.

1905 Roosevelt helps negotiate peace in the Russo-Japanese War.

1906 Roosevelt becomes the first American to win the Nobel Peace Prize. The Preservation of American Antiquities Act is passed. He visits Panama, becoming the first president to leave the United States while in office.

1907 Roosevelt sends the Great White Fleet on a worldwide tour.

1909 Roosevelt embarks on a yearlong African safari.

1910 Roosevelt accepts the Nobel Peace Prize in Christiania, (Oslo) Norway.

1912 Roosevelt accepts the Progressive Party nomination for president. He is shot while campaigning.

1913 Roosevelt writes his autobiography after losing the presidency. He retires and goes on an expedition to explore the source of a river in Brazil.

1915 Roosevelt urges the United States to take action against Germany after the sinking of the *Lusitania.*

1917 Roosevelt asks President Wilson for permission to lead a volunteer regiment to Europe.

1918 Son Quentin is killed in France.

1919 Theodore Roosevelt dies on January 6.

SOURCE NOTES

7 H. W. Brands, ed., *The Selected Letters of Theodore Roosevelt* (New York: Cooper Square Press, 2001), 269.

8 Nathan Miller, *Theodore Roosevelt: A Life* (New York: William Morrow and Company, 1992), 350.

8 Edmund Morris, *Theodore Rex* (New York: Random House, 2001), 6.

10 Edmund Morris, *The Rise of Theodore Roosevelt* (New York: Ballantine Books, 1979), 60.

13 Miller, 32.

13 Theodore Roosevelt, *An Autobiography* (1913; reprint, New York: Da Capo Press, 1985), 29.

16 Miller, 46.

16 Ibid.

17 H. W. Brands, *TR: The Last Romantic* (New York: Basic Books, 1997), 101.

18 Roosevelt, 19.

19 Miller, 55.

20 Ibid., 60.

21 Ibid., 64.

21 Ibid., 67.

22 Morris, *The Rise of Theodore Roosevelt,* 95.

23 Miller, 97.

24 Ibid., 101.

24 Brands, *TR: The Last Romantic,* 107.

27 Kathleen Dalton, *Theodore Roosevelt: A Strenuous Life* (New York: Alfred A. Knopf, 2002), 90.

28 Morris, *The Rise of Theodore Roosevelt,* 153.

29 Ibid., 162.

29 Miller, 123.

29 Morris, *The Rise of Theodore Roosevelt,* 170.

29 Ibid.

31 David McCullough, *Mornings on Horseback* (New York: A Touchstone Book, 1981), 323.

32 Miller, 155.

32 McCullough, 285.

33 Ibid.

34 Ibid., 336.

34 Ibid., 329.

38 Ibid., 348.

39 Morris, *The Rise of Theodore Roosevelt,* 336.

39 Ibid., 337.

40 Brands, *TR: The Last Romantic,* 216.

40 Ibid., 200.

43 Morris, *The Rise of Theodore Roosevelt,* 391.

44 Ibid., 569.

44 Miller, 205.

45 Sylvia Jukes Morris, *Edith Kermit Roosevelt: Portrait of a First Lady* (New York: The Modern Library, 1980), 148.

47 Ibid., 483.

47 Miller, 240.

48 Ibid., 219.

49 Ibid., 266.

49 Brands, *TR: The Last Romantic,* 327.

50 Morris, *Edith Kermit Roosevelt,* 170.

50 Morris, *The Rise of Theodore Roosevelt,* 622.

52 Ibid., 639.

53 Ibid., 654.

53 Peter Collier and David Horowitz, *The Roosevelts: An American Saga* (New York: A Touchstone Book, 1994), 99.

54 Ibid., 100.

55 Morris, *The Rise of Theodore Roosevelt,* 658.

56 Brands, *The Selected Letters of Theodore Roosevelt,* 210.

56 Morris, *The Rise of Theodore Roosevelt,* 662–663.
56 Ibid., 664.
57 Brands, *The Selected Letters of Theodore Roosevelt,* 212.
57 Morris, *The Rise of Theodore Roosevelt,* 664.
57 Ibid.
60 Ibid., 685.
61 Miller, 329.
62 Morris, *The Rise of Theodore Roosevelt,* 702.
63 Ibid., 705.
64 Ibid., 717.
64 Miller, 335.
65 Ibid., 338.
65 Ibid., 340.
67 Dalton, 203.
67 Brands, *TR: The Last Romantic,* 342.
67 Miller, 344.
69 Ibid., 346.
70 Morris, *Theodore Rex,* 11.
71 James MacGregor Burns and Susan Dunn, *The Three Roosevelts: Patrician Leaders Who Transformed America* (New York: Grove Press, 2001), 62.
72 Morris, *Theodore Rex,* 65.
73 George Grant, *Carry a Big Stick: The Uncommon Heroism of Theodore Roosevelt* (Nashville: Cumberland House Publishing, 1996), 119.
74 Morris, *Theodore Rex,* 74.
76 Ibid., 161.
77 Miller, 375.
77 Ibid., 377.
78 Brands, *TR: The Last Romantic,* 290–291.
79 Miller, 435.
79 Ibid., 441.
81 Collier and Horowitz, 118.
82 Morris, *Theodore Rex,* 414.
84 Ibid., 519.
85 Brands, *TR: The Last Romantic,* 557.
87 Miller, 479.
87 Ibid., 481.
88 Ibid., 495.
91 Brands, *TR: The Last Romantic,* 669.
92 Dalton, 360.
93 Miller, 522.
95 Ibid., 530.
95 Brands, *TR: The Last Romantic,* 721.
96 Miller, 535.
96 Ibid., 538.
96 Ibid., 546.
97 Burns and Dunn, 147.
98 Miller, 557.
100 Ibid., 564.
100 Ibid.
100 Ibid., 556.
100 Ibid., 566.
102 Edward J. Renehen Jr., *The Lion's Pride: Theodore Roosevelt and His Family in Peace and War* (New York: Oxford University Press, 1999), 223.
102 Roosevelt, 372.
103 Renehen, 222.

SELECTED BIBLIOGRAPHY

Auchincloss, Louis. *Theodore Roosevelt.* New York: Times Books, 2001.

Barone, Michael. "A Big Stick: TR's Sure Sense of America Has Much to Tell Us Today." *U.S. News and World Report* 132, no. 6 (2002): 52–58.

Brands, H. W., ed. *The Selected Letters of Theodore Roosevelt.* New York: Cooper Square Press, 2001.

———. *TR: The Last Romantic.* New York: Basic Books, 1997.

Burns, James MacGregor, and Susan Dunn. *The Three Roosevelts: Patrician Leaders Who Transformed America.* New York: Grove Press, 2001.

Collier, Peter, and David Horowitz. *The Roosevelts: An American Saga.* New York: A Touchstone Book, 1994.

Dalton, Kathleen. *Theodore Roosevelt: A Strenuous Life.* New York: Alfred A. Knopf, 2002.

Grant, George. *Carry a Big Stick: The Uncommon Heroism of Theodore Roosevelt.* Nashville: Cumberland House Publishing, 1996.

McCullough, David. *Mornings on Horseback.* New York: A Touchstone Book, 1981.

Miller, Nathan. *Theodore Roosevelt: A Life.* New York: William Morrow and Company, 1992.

Morris, Edmund. *The Rise of Theodore Roosevelt.* New York: Ballantine Books, 1979.

———. *Theodore Rex.* New York: Random House, 2001.

Morris, Sylvia Jukes. *Edith Kermit Roosevelt: Portrait of a First Lady.* New York: The Modern Library, 1980.

Renehan, Edward J., Jr. *The Lion's Pride: Theodore Roosevelt and His Family in Peace and War.* New York: Oxford University Press, 1999.

Roosevelt, Theodore. *An Autobiography.* 1913. Reprint, New York: Da Capo Press, 1985.

———. *A Bully Father: Theodore Roosevelt's Letters to His Children.* Edited by Joan Paterson Kerr. New York: Random House, 1995.

———. *Theodore Roosevelt's Diaries of Boyhood and Youth.* New York: Charles Scribner's Sons, 1928.

FURTHER READING AND WEBSITES

Armstrong, Jennifer. *Dear Mr. President: Theodore Roosevelt, Letters from a Young Coal Miner.* New York: Winslow Press, 2001.

Fritz, Jean. *Bully for You, Teddy Roosevelt!* New York: Penguin Putnam Books for Young Readers, 1991.

Kraft, Betsy Harvey. *Theodore Roosevelt: Champion of the American Spirit.* New York: Clarion Books, 2003.

Mt. Rushmore: Presidents on the Rocks. <http://t3.preservice.org/T0211461/roosevelt/>. This website includes "fun facts" on Theodore Roosevelt, a list of children's books, and links to other websites.

Sagamore Hill. <http://www.liglobal.com/t_i/saghill/>. This website includes information on Roosevelt's life and family as well as a layout of his famous house.

Weitzman, David. *The Mountain Man and the President.* New York: Steck-Vaughn, 1993.

INDEX

ABOUT THE AUTHOR

Stephanie Sammartino McPherson, a former high school teacher, has written many newspaper and magazine stories and many books for children, including *Wilbur & Orville Wright, Jonas Salk,* and *Liberty or Death.* Stephanie and her husband, Richard, live in Virginia but also call California home.

———————— ✧ ————————

PHOTO ACKNOWLEDGMENTS

The images in this book are used with the permission of: The White House, pp. 1, 7, 10, 17, 27, 34, 44, 57, 67, 91; Library of Congress, pp. 2 [LC-USZ62-7220], 12 [LC-USZ62-132504], 13 [LC-USZC4-1755], 19 [LC-USZ62-118798], 22 [LC-USZ62-23232], 23 [LC-USZ62-25802], 31 [LC-USZ62-091125], 35 [LC-USZ62-94192], 36 [LC-USZ62-93845], 37 [LC-USZ62-25803], 39 [LC-USZ62-96286], 42 [LC-USZ62-13023], 48 [LC-USZ62-80], 51 [LC-USZ62-127283], 58 [LC-BH832-1329], 59 [LC-USZ62-95887], 61 [LC-USZ62-122402], 62 [LC-USZ62-22198], 66 [LC-USZ62-100475], 68 [LC-USZ62-96930], 69 [LC-USZ62-5377], 70 [LC-USZ62-96529], 71 [LC-USZ62-5512], 72 [LC-USZ62-96241], 78 [LC-D4-73205], 79 [LC-USZ62-98438], 85 [LC-USZ62-32857], 86 [LC-USZ62-85403], 93 [LC-USZ62-089631]; Yosemite National Park Research Library, p. 6; Theodore Roosevelt Collection, Harvard College Library, pp. 11, 45; Image by Will Dunniway, p. 18; Harvard University Graduate School of Design, Frances Loeb Library, p. 21; National Archives, pp. 25 [W&C 87], 52 [W&C 299]; Brown Brothers, pp. 28, 46, 64, 80, 87, 90, 94, 97, 99, 102; Hayden Survey, U.S. Geological Survey Photo Library, p. 41; courtesy Frederic Remington Art Museum, Ogdensburg, New York, p. 53; © Bettmann/CORBIS, p. 55; The Boston Journal, p. 73; © North Wind Picture Archives, pp. 75, 76, 82; U.S. Fish & Wildlife Service, p. 84; © Jim Simondet/Independent Picture Service, p. 89; © Finley Holiday Films, p. 101.

Cover: Library of Congress [LC-USZ62-106668].